[iNSiDE]

Chetham's Library

THE BUILDING

CHETHAM'S MEDIEVAL ROOTS

Chetham's sits on a sandstone outcrop at the confluence of the Rivers Irwell and Irk, a site of strategic importance that has been occupied since Roman times. The present building dates from the second quarter of the fifteenth century. In 1421 Thomas de la Warre, Lord of Manchester and rector of the parish church, obtained a licence from Henry V to transform the church into a college with a warden, eight fellows, four clerks and six lay choristers.

De la Warre gave up his own manor house and land for the impressive new building, which was erected from local sandstone, quarried in Collyhurst and brought to the site by river barge. The generous accommodation included a large hall, the warden's own lodgings and a set of rooms for each of the fellows. In addition, the complex had its own bakehouse, brewery and stables, as well as ample domestic facilities and guest rooms. Other than the church, it was the largest building in the medieval town of Manchester.

The survival of such a complete medieval domestic building is rare, and its troubled history makes that survival even more surprising. In 1547 the College was dissolved, and the Earl of Derby acquired the property as a town residence. The College was re-founded, closed down and then re-opened, but gradually fell into disrepair until its restoration as the site for Humphrey Chetham's legacy.

View from the River Irk, 1831.

Right: Chetham's College, Manchester, from a drawing by John Palmer, *c.* 1815.

Below: The medieval buildings with courtyard, as seen today.

CLOISTER COURT

The three-sided cloister is arranged around a small, cobbled courtyard. You can still see the stone doorways that led to the fellows' rooms, some with their medieval wooden doors. All the ground-floor rooms had a fireplace and were of a generous size. The lower walkway probably had a dirt floor covered in rushes, and the windows were unglazed. The stone floor and glazing date from the rebuilding work in the 1650s.

Unusually, the cloister has two storeys, and the upper gallery once gave access to the fellows' bed chambers. The staircase to the first floor was originally in the northwest corner, moving to the northeast in the seventeenth century. The Library now occupies the west and south ranges of the cloister, and a new entrance and staircase were inserted in the southwest corner in the 1870s by Alfred Waterhouse.

The courtyard has become known as Fox Court, owing to an optical illusion: on looking through one of the three openings at the top of the old stone well, the light through the other two is reflected in the water, giving the impression that you are staring into the eyes of an animal.

Opposite: View of ground-floor cloister.

Left: Doorway from the library to the north cloister gallery, *c.* 1890.

Above: Seventeenth-century staircase leading to the first-floor gallery, *c.* 1890.

Left: Audit Room with Humphrey Chetham's chair.

Below: Audit Room, from a drawing by John Palmer, c. 1815.

AUDIT ROOM

This is one of the most richly decorated rooms in the building and was originally allocated to the warden of the medieval college. The most notable feature is the timber ceiling, which is divided into nine panels by moulded ribs decorated with wooden bosses. The most grotesque is a Mouth of Hell, with a sinner ensnared in its jaws. The bosses date from the second half of the fifteenth century, and there are some similarities with the panels in the roof of the choir of Manchester Cathedral.

The room was remodelled in the seventeenth century to incorporate elaborate plasterwork, oak panelling and new doors. The current furniture includes a three-legged chair said to have belonged to Humphrey Chetham and some carved panel-back chairs typical of northern England. There are also various eighteenth-century items: a set of twelve ladder-back mahogany chairs and a handsome walnut settee with cabriole legs resting on ball-and-claw feet. The Elizabethan one-fingered lantern clock was presented to Chetham's in 1869.

The large oak refectory table bears a strange mark in one corner, which legend says represents the devil's hoof print. In 1595 John Dee was appointed as warden of the College. Dee was a learned scientist, astronomer, mathematician and advisor to Queen Elizabeth I, but also had a reputation as an alchemist and a student of the occult. The devil is supposed to have materialised over the table and left behind the mark of his hoof while Dee was in pursuit of these more arcane endeavours.

Medieval ceiling boss showing a sinner being consumed by the Mouth of Hell.

READING ROOM

Also part of the warden's accommodation, this room now contains some of the most beautiful furniture in the building. There is a very large gate-leg table and a set of twenty-four leather-backed chairs with oak frames, square backs and turned legs connected by a stretcher carved with scroll work. Both the table and chairs were purchased in the 1650s for the use of the feoffees (Chetham's trustees). The two other tables in the room were probably made for the Library in the 1650s by the local joiner Richard Martinscroft, who was also responsible for making the presses and library stools.

Above the fireplace is a portrait of Humphrey Chetham, the only near-contemporary portrait of the founder. Surrounding this is an elaborate heraldic and emblematic display commemorating Chetham and his foundation. His coat of arms features in the centre, flanked by obelisks resting on books and supporting torches symbolic of learning. To the left is a cock and to the right a pelican in piety, a traditional symbol of Christ's sacrifice.

The walnut tall-case clock is the first recorded gift of an ex-pupil. It was donated in 1695 by Nicholas Clegg, who left Chetham's in 1689 and set up in business as an instrument maker. The clockmaker was Thomas Aynsworth of Westminster, and the barometer set in the door was made by John Patrick of London.

Portrait of Humphrey Chetham above the fireplace in the Reading Room with surrounding carved tympanum.

North end of the Baronial Hall with fifteenth-century wooden screens.

BARONIAL HALL

The Baronial Hall is a wonderfully preserved example of the timber-roofed halls that would have been common in the North West of England, and is comparable in size with Ordsall Hall, Salford, and Rufford Old Hall, Lancashire. The magnificent timber-beamed roof once accommodated a louvre opening to let out smoke from a central hearth. At some point during the sixteenth or seventeenth centuries this was replaced by a simple fireplace with a shallow lintel, which was converted in the nineteenth century into the large inglenook fireplace still there today.

The medieval floor would have been made of earth covered with straw or rushes. The current stone-flagged floor dates from the seventeenth century, as in the cloister. The Baronial Hall retains the beautiful oak screen of three equal sections, of which the central part was originally moveable but is now fixed. The purpose of the screen was to keep out draughts and to conceal the entrances to the buttery and pantry situated at the back of the space. At the top of the Hall an impressive oak canopy projects over a raised dais, where the warden and visiting dignitaries would have dined at high table.

Benefactions
Benefactions
Endowments

Opposite: The old kitchen today with boards recording twentieth-century benefactions from Chetham's Old Boys' Association.

Left: Kitchen interior, *c.* 1900.

THE OLD KITCHEN AND BUTTERY

This impressive double-storey room was until recently the kitchen of the College and School. Lit by two lines of windows facing the courtyard, it contains the remains of two fireplaces on the north and east walls. The larger, in the north wall, has a fine lintel with a tall relieving arch, above which are hung some examples of cooking equipment. Recesses in the walls would have been used to store food.

At the northern end of the Baronial Hall are two doors that would have led into a pantry and buttery. These rooms were knocked into one in the nineteenth century to make a separate staff dining room, which contains an ornate Victorian Gothic Revival oak dining table and chairs.

There is an extensive network of cellars below these rooms, which at one time gave access to the River Irk, an important transport link and source of fish in the early days of the building's history. Early drawings of this aspect of the College building show steps leading down to the riverbank and a boathouse. One of these cellars was known as the 'snake pit', probably due to the presence of eels, which emerged from the river at high water.

THE HISTORY

HUMPHREY CHETHAM

Born in 1580 in Crumpsall near Manchester, Humphrey Chetham was the most successful gentleman merchant of seventeenth-century Lancashire. He made his fortune in the cloth trade, mainly buying and selling fustian, a strong woven fabric made of linen and cotton. In the 1620s he began to purchase land and property in the Manchester area and later lived at Clayton Hall near Droylsden.

For many years before his death, Chetham attempted to make provision for a large charitable scheme. His concern was to overcome poverty by curing ignorance, and through education provide the hope of a livelihood for underprivileged boys. The school he founded was known as Chetham's Hospital because it was a place of shelter and instruction. Chetham died unmarried on 20 September 1653 at the age of 72 and was buried amid much pomp and ceremony at the Collegiate Church of Manchester (now Manchester Cathedral).

The first task facing his executors was to purchase the medieval College House, which, after many years of neglect, was in a poor state. During the Civil War it had been used as a prison and arsenal, and it was remarked that 'the towne swine make there abode bothe in the yards and house'.

Left: Coat of arms granted to Humphrey Chetham in 1635.

Opposite: Portrait of Humphrey Chetham by an unknown artist, oil on panel, c. 1700.

Left: The Priests' Wing, which originally housed the College priests' bedrooms.

Above: Detail showing locking system for rods and chains.

Opposite: Carved stool with S-shaped hand-holds.

THE CREATION OF THE LIBRARY

Humphrey Chetham's will of 1651 stipulated that the Library should be 'for the use of schollars and others well affected'. Richard Martinscroft was employed to fit out and furnish the Library, which was housed on the first floor for better daylight and to avoid rising damp. The books were chained to the bookcases, or presses, in accordance with Chetham's instructions. Twenty-four carved oak stools with S-shaped hand-holds were provided as portable seats for readers.

In 1655 three feoffees were nominated to select books for the Library. Most of the early acquisitions were bought from a single London bookseller and packed into barrels to protect them on their journey north. In the first thirty years, the Library bought mainly books on theology, law, history, medicine and science. The aim was to build up as quickly as possible a collection that would meet the needs of the clergy, lawyers and doctors of Manchester and the surrounding towns.

By the mid-eighteenth century the Library's collection had outgrown the original shelves, and the presses were increased in height. The practice of chaining was abandoned and, instead, gates were put up to prevent theft. From then on, material was brought to the Reading Room for study, a practice that continues today. The system of alphabetically labelling each press can still be seen on the oak panels, along with traces of the early hinges and plates for the chains. This fixed location system is still used today, in conjunction with the modern electronic catalogue.

HUMPHREY CHETHAM'S PARISH LIBRARIES

Under the terms of Chetham's will, the sum of £200 was allocated for the provision of five small libraries to be placed in the parish churches of Manchester, Bolton, Gorton, Turton and Walmsley. The feoffees were instructed to purchase 'godly Englishe Bookes ... for the edification of the common people'. The books were to be chained to prevent their removal and housed in wooden chests. The library at Gorton, the first to be completed, contained fifty-one works and cost nearly £33.

The books are shelved with the fore-edge rather than the spine facing outwards to prevent the chains from rubbing against the bindings with use. Originally a long sloping shelf in front of and immediately below the doors would have served to rest volumes on when in use.

Of the five parish libraries, only those of Gorton and Turton survive. In 1984 the chained library of Gorton was placed in Chetham's Library on permanent loan and was bought outright with the help of a National Lottery grant in 2001.

Left: The library of the Parish Church of St James Gorton, 1655.

Opposite: Books, fore-edge out and chained, from the Gorton Parish Library.

THE LIBRARY'S COLLECTIONS

PRINTED BOOKS

There are over 120,000 printed items, of which more than half were published before 1850. While there are many important individual texts, the collection is more significant because of how and when the books came into the Library. In many instances it is known who owned particular books, and also when, why and from whom they were acquired; how the Library shelved, arranged and organised them; how they were listed, catalogued and made available; and, finally, who read them once they were here. Beyond the famous names lie many hundreds of other owners whose names, annotations and inscriptions are now available for study through the Library's catalogues.

In the fields of theology, classical literature and history, Chetham's holdings of early printed books are both comprehensive in their coverage and rich in their depth. The foundation collection also includes important works on a range of other subjects, notably architecture, bibliography, heraldry, law, numismatics, technology and applied science.

Library books, some stamped with the Griffin from Chetham's coat of arms.

Quita etas mundi Folium LXXVI

Demas philosophus atheniensis alexandri tempe claruit. Hic dum alexāder obtinere vellet ⁊ obsideret Athenas restitit: psuadens atheniēn. vt non tradere[n]t ei ciuitatem. Tandē alexandro ciuitate obtenta demas ei adhesit alexandro exhibēs se familiarē. Verū atheniēsibus alexandro sacrificare volētibus: dixit. videte ne dum celū custoditis terram āmittatis: huius dematis dictum fuit. Amico mutuā me erogante pecuniam: ipm et pecuniam perdam.

Quintus Curcius pbus increpauit alexandrum eo q sibi optabat adhiberi diuinos honores. d. Si deus es largire nobis beneficia immortalitatis ⁊ nō auferas. Si homo semp id cogita aliis postposit[is].

In diebus quibus Alexander natus est: diris prodigiis romani territi fuerūt. Nam sol visus est pugnasse cum luna. Saxa sanguinē sudauerunt: in die plures lune apparuerunt in celo. Nox vsq; ad plurimam diei partem tendi visa est tunc et saxa de nubibus cecidere. et p septem dies grando lapideis immixtis ⁊ te

Annotations by Thomas Gudlawe of Wigan in the *Nuremberg Chronicle*, 1493.

One of the first books acquired, an eleven-volume set of the works of St Augustine, for the price of £7, was the starting point for a very large and varied library of theology. There is a good collection of Bibles, including all four of the great Polyglot (multilingual) editions from the sixteenth and seventeenth centuries. The feoffees were prepared to spend vast sums of money on particularly desirable volumes, paying as much as £20, for example, for an eight-volume Bible. By comparison, the first Chetham's librarian was paid £10, plus board and lodging, for a year's work.

The scientific collections are especially significant: works by Aristotle, Euclid, Galileo, Copernicus and Kepler were all acquired at the outset, as were other outstanding volumes on natural history and medicine, notably early editions of Galen and Hippocrates. The feoffees were also interested in the new science, and bought first editions of Robert Hooke's *Micrographia* (1665) and Isaac Newton's *Principia Mathematica* (1687).

By the mid-eighteenth century the Library also began to acquire large illustrated works and multi-volume periodicals and journals. A century later the emphasis shifted again. Until the nineteenth century Chetham's had been the only repository for books and printed matter in Manchester, but with the creation of rate-supported public libraries, the feoffees agreed that the policy of buying books on all subjects could no longer be sustained. Instead, the decision was made to specialise in the history and topography of the North West of England. Chetham's now has one of the largest collections of material relating to Manchester and its region, with extensive holdings of prints, maps

English Botany by James Edward Smith and James Sowerby, 1790–1814.

and photographic slides, and large runs of newspapers, trade directories and periodicals.

As a major rare book repository and a nationally significant centre for the study of history, it is essential that the Library continues to develop its collections relating to the North West, and to fill gaps in its older historic collections. Material is still being added by purchase and by donation. In the twenty-first century, for example, we have acquired the Eddie Cass collection of Manchester fiction and books from the Manchester Region Industrial Archaeology Society.

Above: Books from the Cass collection.

Left: *Philosophical Transactions* of the Royal Society.

Belle Vue Gardens: Official Guide.

MANUSCRIPTS AND ARCHIVES

The Library has collected manuscripts and archives since the 1650s when it built up an impressive collection of medieval manuscripts, including the thirteenth-century *Flores Historiarum* of Matthew Paris and an important early compendium of Middle English poetry. By the end of the eighteenth century, however, Chetham's was increasingly seen as a repository for local records, indeed the only proper repository for public papers in the region until the twentieth century. Many of the local manuscripts and archival holdings came to Chetham's in the second half of the nineteenth century, often through members of local historical societies, particularly the Chetham Society.

The manuscript and archival collections are mainly concerned with the history of the North West of England. There are extensive collections of title deeds, institutional records and antiquarian papers collected and compiled by local historians. There is the oldest history of Manchester (Richard Hollingworth's 1656 *Mancuniensis*), the first ever census of Manchester (compiled in 1773–74) and numerous social, economic and political papers, including wage books of early mills, and accounts of the poorhouse and overseers of the poor.

One of the largest institutional collections concerns Belle Vue Zoo and Pleasure Gardens, founded in 1836 on the eastern side of the city. As well as being the country's most important provincial zoo, Belle Vue was also famous for hosting firework displays, concerts, brass band contests, ballroom dancing and political meetings, and for its amusement park, circus and speedway.

Coronation of Edward the Confessor from the *Flores Historiarum* of Matthew Paris, mid-13th–early 14th century.

Political ephemera from
the Robert Hay scrapbook.

Above: **'Manchester Ballad Seller'**, from the Earl of Ellesmere's scrapbook.

Right: *The Cotton Spinners Solicitation* ballad from the Halliwell-Phillipps collection.

A WINDOW INTO EVERYDAY LIFE

In addition to printed books, archives and manuscripts, Chetham's has an enormous amount of ephemera, with particularly rich collections of postcards, chapbooks, broadsides, ballads, theatre programmes, posters, trade cards and bill heads. Many of these were given to the Library in 1852 by the Shakespearean scholar James Orchard Halliwell-Phillipps. His collection of over 3,100 items contains many unique works: fragments of medieval manuscripts; sixteenth-century black-letter ballads; political, social and commercial broadsides; and songs and music dating from 1680 to 1750.

There are many albums and scrapbooks of local material, including rare specimens of Manchester printing. One album, for example, known as the 'Cambrics Scrapbook', contains over 250 broadsheets, ranging from light-hearted entertainment handbills to notices of serious political issues, mostly dating from the end of the eighteenth century. Another work, the 'Manchester Scrapbook', was compiled by the Earl of Ellesmere and given to the Library in 1838. This large work contains almost 400 items, including pen-and-ink sketches of local characters, scenes and customs.

The Cotton Spinners Solicitation,
A NEW SONG.
Tune,---" Bumkin's Journey to London."

Wooden common press presented to the Library in 1900 by the printer George Falkner and Sons, Deansgate Press.

A CABINET OF CURIOSITIES

For much of its history Chetham's was also home to a bizarre collection of curiosities, including a woman's skeleton, an alligator's skin, a young swordfish, a flying stag, the tail of a rattlesnake, an ostrich egg, two coconuts, a large calabash, a branch of white coral, a lodestone, a tortoise shell, a hummingbird and an enormous stone taken out of a woman's bladder. Some, however, were completely fanciful: a boot worn by Queen Elizabeth, Oliver Cromwell's sword and arrows belonging to Robin Hood.

The collection featured in some of Manchester's first guidebooks and made the Library something of a tourist attraction not long after its foundation. The writer Celia Fiennes visited Manchester in 1698 and claimed: 'There I saw the skinn of a rattle snake 6 foote long with many other Curiositys, their anatomy of a man wired together, and the jaw of a sherke.'

In the nineteenth century, visiting the Library's museum became, for some, part of their wedding arrangements. A local ballad, *Johnny Green's Wedding and Description of Manchester College*, recounts the practice by which Oldham couples would walk into Manchester on Easter Monday in large numbers to marry at the Collegiate Church. Afterwards the wedding party, most of whom were the worse for wear from drink, would tour the College to marvel at the curiosities on display.

The Library is still home to many objects and artworks, but almost all of the more unusual curiosities were removed at the beginning of the twentieth century and given to Salford Museum.

Reading Room, from a drawing by John Palmer, c. 1815.

MARX AND ENGELS

The great radical philosopher and father of communism, Karl Marx, spent time studying at Chetham's Library during the middle years of the nineteenth century. Marx's first visit to Manchester took place in the summer of 1845 when he was conducting research for his book on political economy. His friend and close collaborator, Friedrich Engels, was employed from 1842 to 1869 at his father's Salford cotton-manufacturing firm, working his way up from office clerk to joint proprietor. Although Engels disliked the work, it enabled him to offer financial support to Marx and his family, who had very little income. Marx observed at first hand the appalling living conditions of the working classes in the tightly packed streets and alleyways of the city.

Evidently the Library made a strong impression on the two men. Writing to Marx in 1870 Engels commented: 'During the last few days I have again spent a good deal of time sitting at the four-sided desk in the alcove where we sat together twenty-four years ago. I am very fond of the place. The stained glass window ensures that the weather is always fine there. Old Jones, the Librarian, is still alive but he is very old and no longer active. I have not seen him on this occasion.'

The desk where Marx and Engels sat together remains in the Reading Room alcove, and the books they consulted in 1845 are still held by the Library.

THE FUTURE

Chetham's Hospital, School and Library remains an independent charity and continues to be administered by twenty-four feoffees. We are home to three remarkable institutions – Chetham's School of Music, Chetham's Library and Stoller Hall – united by a shared vision: to bring people together through music, learning and culture.

Thanks to their uninterrupted stewardship and management over four centuries, Chetham's Library collections are far more valuable to the scholar than many larger libraries that have been assembled privately. In few other places can the growth of an historic library be studied in such depth, through such a wealth of materials and in surroundings so appropriate.

Alcove desk with facsimiles of books consulted by Marx and Engels in 1845.

First published in 2025 by
Kulturalis Ltd
14 Old Queen Street
London SW1H 9HP
United Kingdom
www.kulturalis.com

In association with
Chetham's Library
Long Millgate
Manchester M3 1SB

ISBN 978-1-83636-037-7

Project manager and copy-editor: Catherine Hooper
Designer: Matthew Wilson
Printed and bound in Turkey
Reproduction by Opero, Verona

10 9 8 7 6 5 4 3 2 1

British Library Cataloguing in Publication Data. A catalogue record for this book is available from the British Library.

EU GPSR Authorised Representative:
EASY ACCESS SYSTEM EUROPE OÜ, Mustamäe tee 50,
10621, TALLINN, Estonia
email: info@easproject.org

Front cover: Mary Chapel Wing of the Library.

Back cover (clockwise from top left): Portrait of Humphrey Chetham (p. 15), the medieval building (p. 3), wooden common press (pp. 28–9) and library books (p. 20).

Inside front cover: Library press showing alphabetical location system.

Inside back cover: *The South West Prospect of Manchester and Salford* by Robert Whitworth (hand-coloured), 1734. Chetham's is visible to the left of the Cathedral, on the extreme left of the prospect.